Travel Journal for Kids:
All The Places We Can Go!

Copyright© 2023 by Bookfly Publishing

No part of this publication may be reproduced, stored in a retrieval system, or transmitted in any form or by any means, electronic, mechanical, photocopying, recording, or otherwise, without the written permission of the publisher. Limited Liability/Disclaimer of Warranty. The publisher and the author make no representation or warranties with the respect to the accuracy or completeness of the contents of this work and specifically disclaim all warranties including without limitation warranties for a particular purpose. No warranty may be created or extended by sales or promotional materials. The advice or strategies contained herein may not be suitable for every situation. This work is sold with the understanding that the publisher is not engaged in rendering medical, legal, or other professional advice or services. Neither the publisher nor the author or creator shall be liable for damages arising.

Cover Designer: Uliana Barabash

For general information on our other products and services please visit www.bookflypublishing.com or contact us at info@bookflypublishing.com.
Bookfly Publishing publishes its books and materials in a variety of electronic and print formats. Some content that appears in print may not be available in electronic books and vice versa.

ISBN 978-1-7369393-6-9
All rights reserved. Published by Bookfly Publishing
Harvey, Louisiana
www.bookflypublishing.com

Printed in the USA

ALL THE

Where would you like to go?
What states have you traveled to?
Which is your favorite state to visit?

PLACES WE CAN GO!

The United States of America

The Continents

CKET LIST

our travel bucket list
ou want to go and see

Things I Want to See

 # Packing Checklist

☐ underwear

☐ sleepwear

☐ swimwear

☐ socks

☐ jeans

☐ shirt

☐ dress

☐ hoodie

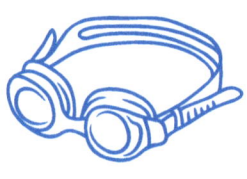
☐ goggles

☐ snorkel

☐ cap / hat

☐ sunglasses

☐ sneakers

☐ hiking boots

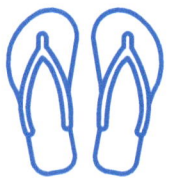
☐ flipflops / sandals

Packing Checklist

☐ towel

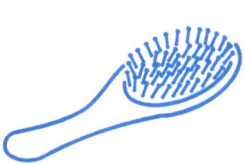
☐ hair brush

☐ body wash

☐ shampoo & conditioner

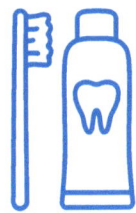
☐ toothbrush & toothpaste

☐ mouthwash & dental floss

☐ eyedrops

☐ sunscreen

☐ hand sanitizer

☐ wipes

☐ bug spray

☐ lotion

☐ backpack

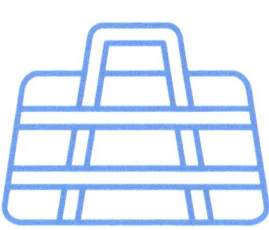
☐ overnight bag

☐ zip-top plastic bag

Trip Date: _____

Destination: _____

Weather Conditions:

Traveled By:

Feeling:

Trip Goals:

1. _____ ☑
2. _____ ☐
3. _____ ☐
4. _____ ☐
5. _____ ☐

Top 3 Trip Goals

1. _____
2. _____
3. _____

Notes:
_____
_____
_____
_____

Trip Activities:

_____
_____
_____
_____

Top 3 Activities:

1. _____
2. _____
3. _____

Notes:

_____
_____
_____
_____

Food Places Visited During Trip: RATING

_____

Notes:

List your favorite food, activity, and goal that you completed or explored on the trip.

BON APPETIT!

Draw a picture of the best food item you ate on the trip

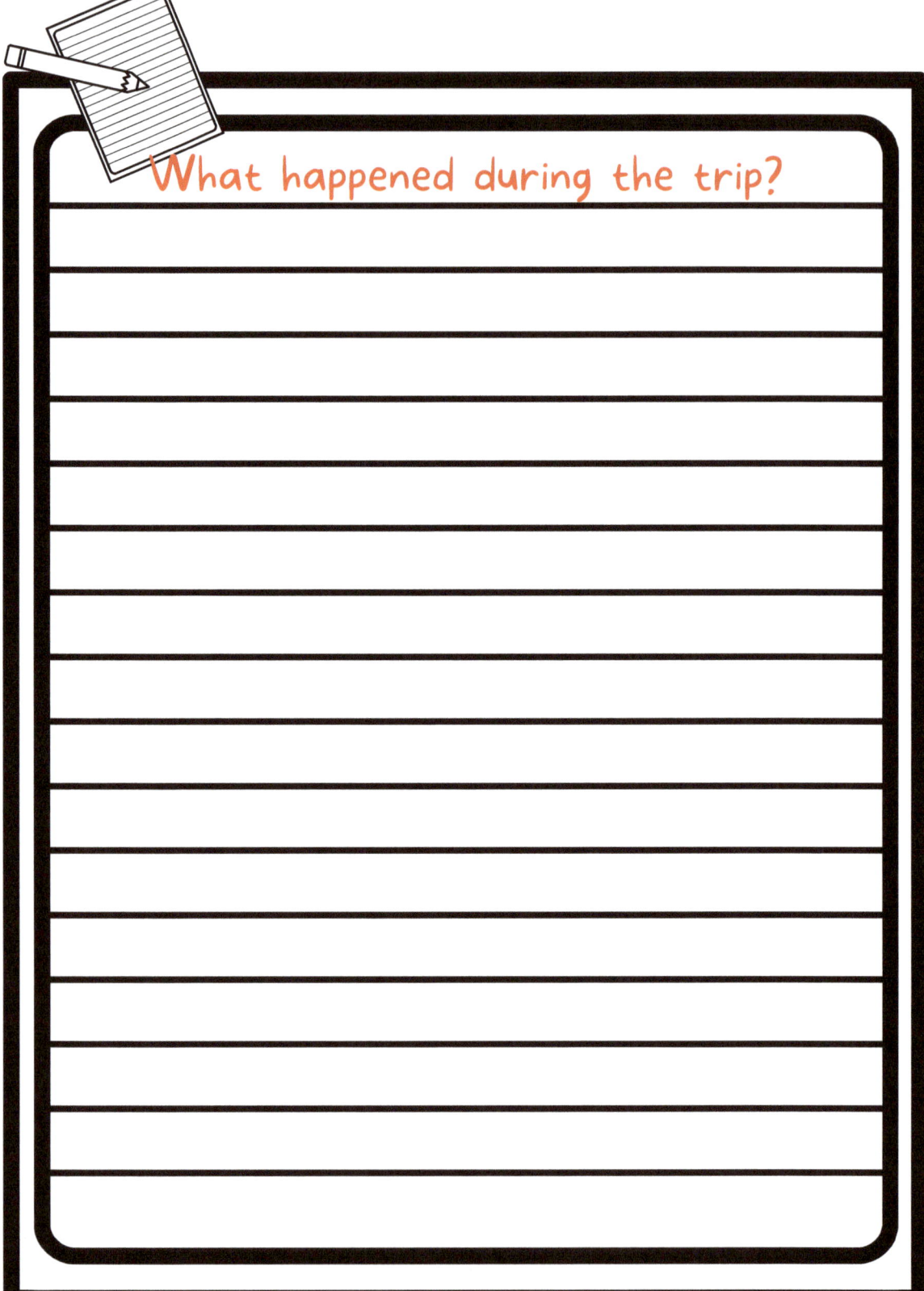

What was the best part of the trip?

TRIP

Places I Went:

Things I Learned

SUMMARY

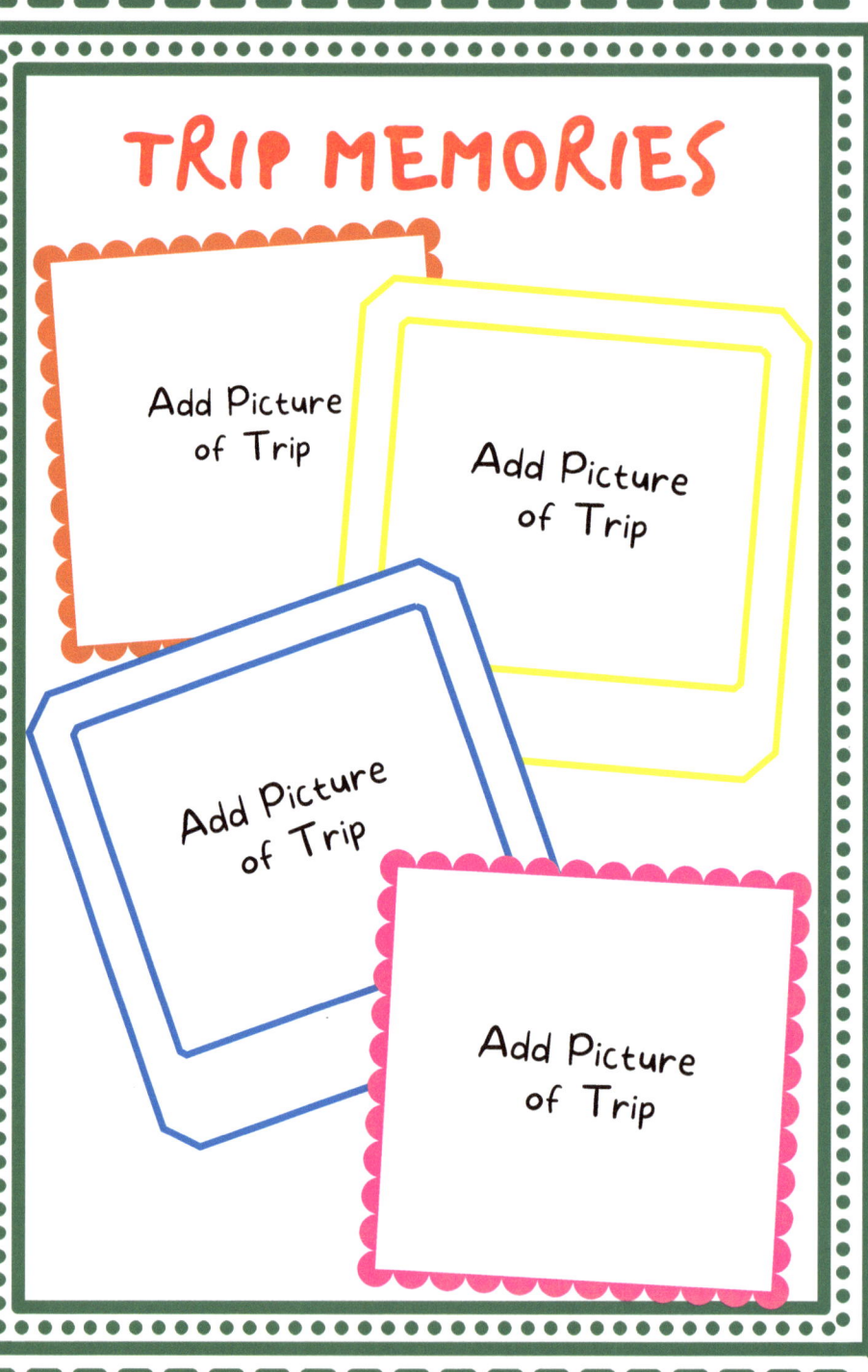

SCRAPBOARD

BEGIN!

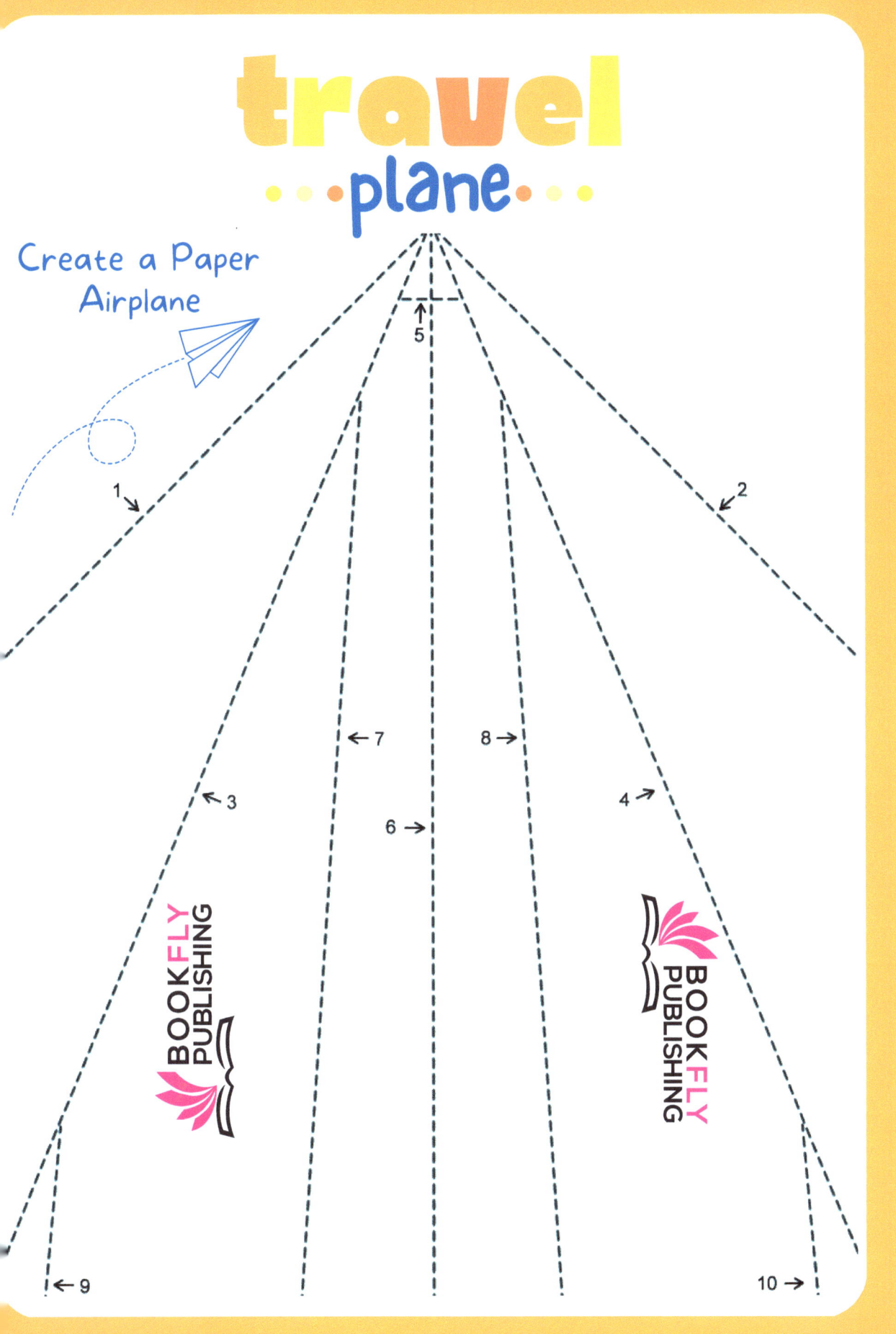

travel
tic tac toe

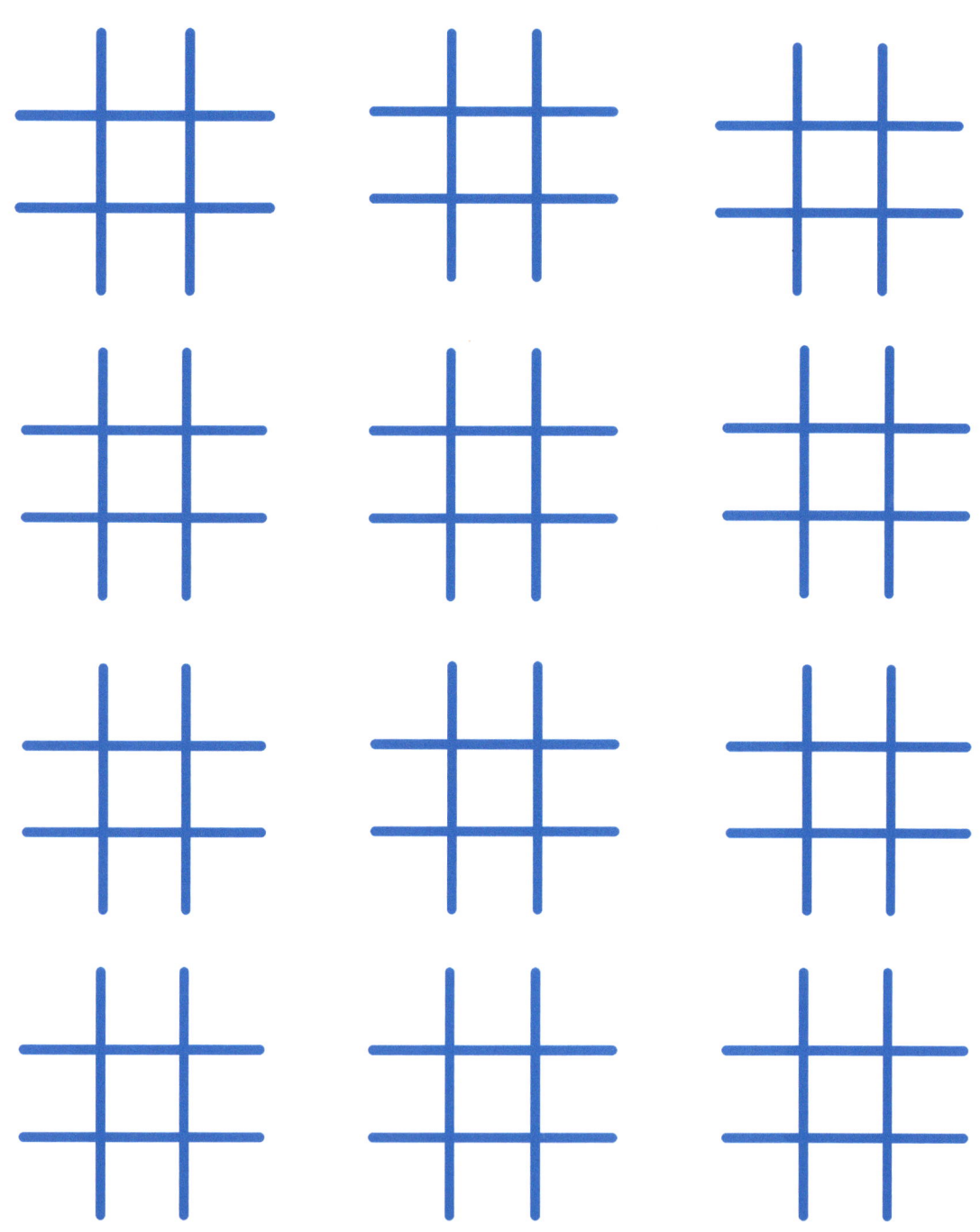

travel
...maze...

See if you can get all your luggage onto the plane.

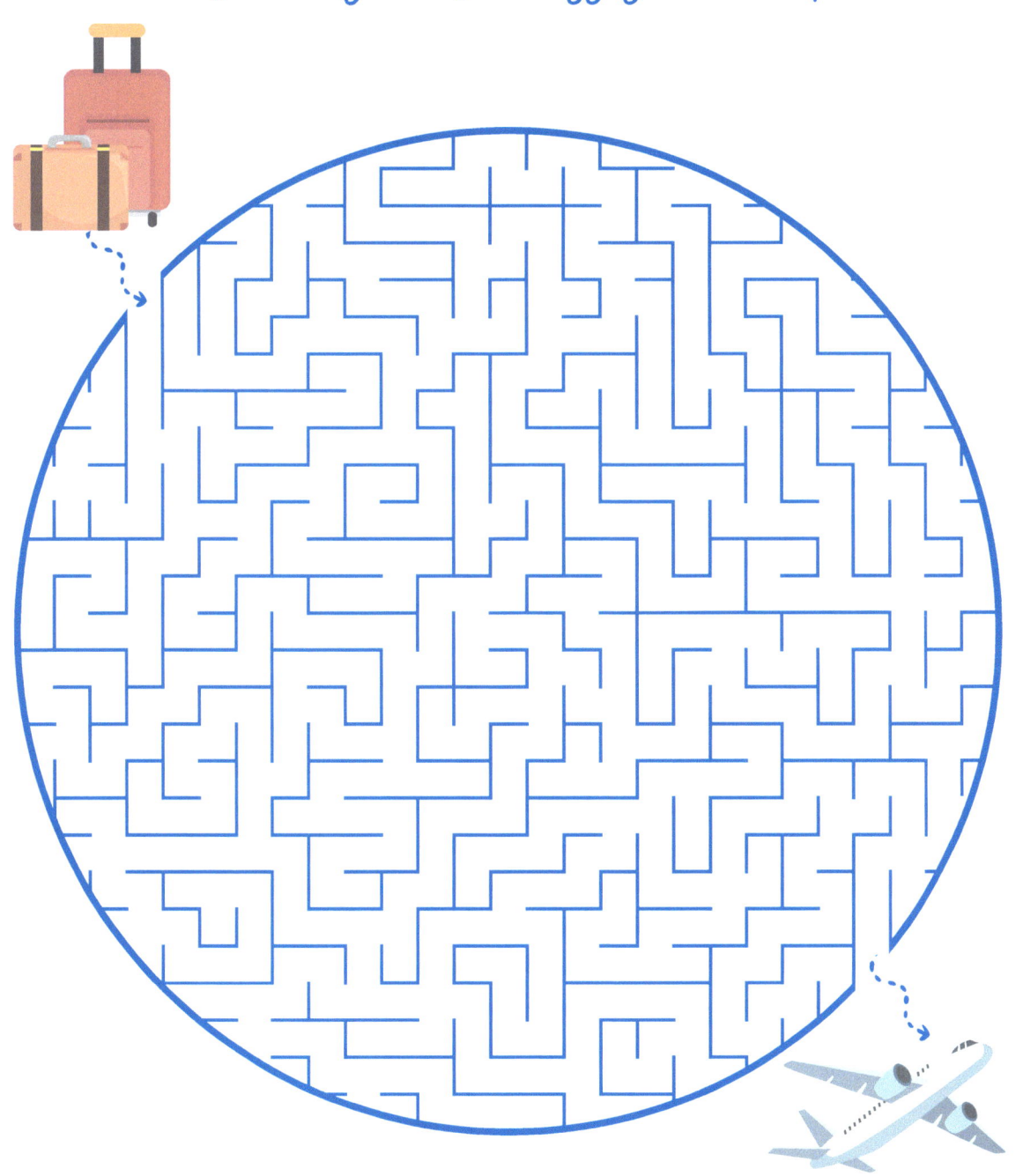

travel
drawing

Draw the other side to finish the picture.

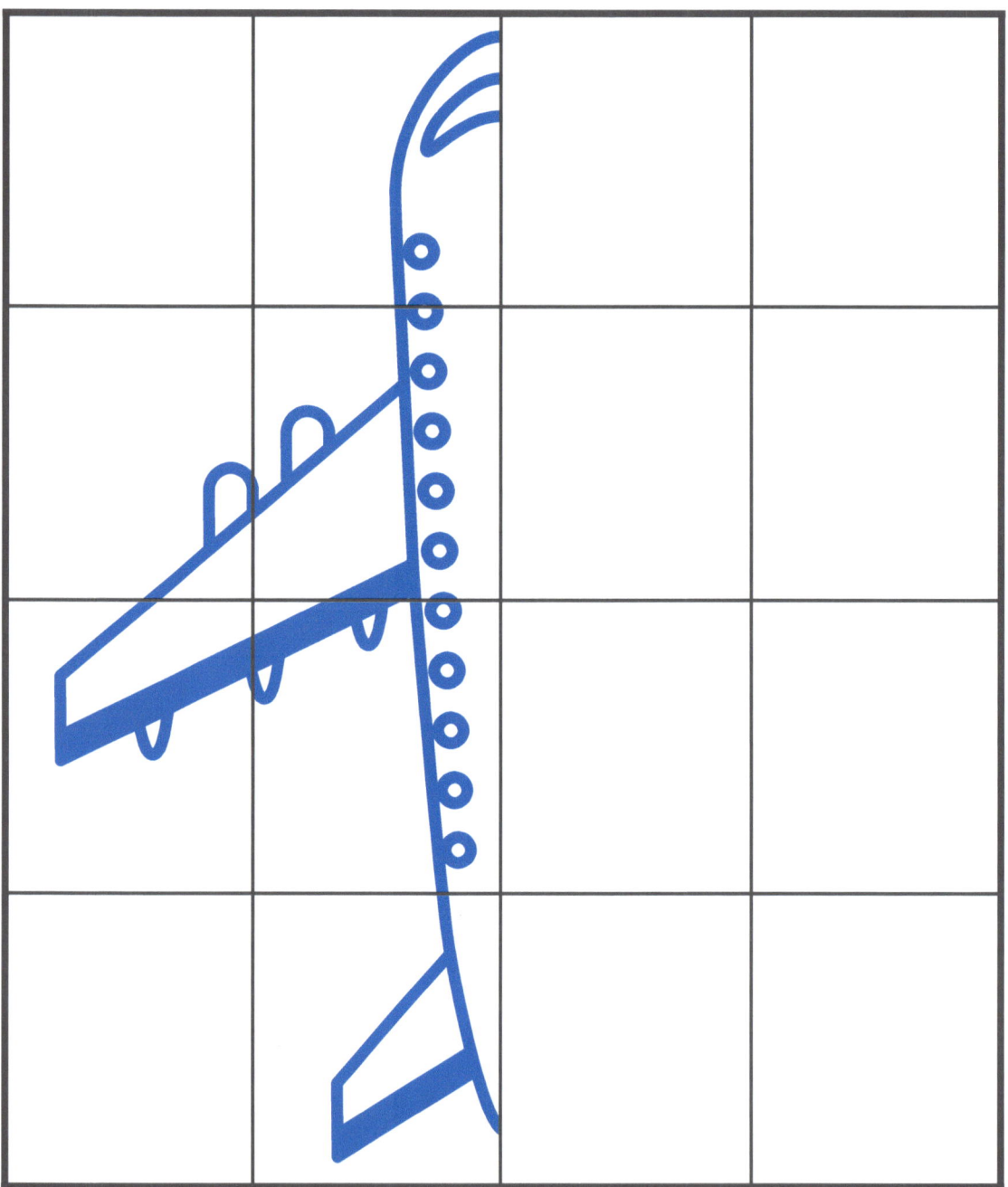

travel
I-SPY signs

See how many of each item you can find.

travel
···scavenger hunt···

Every time you see one of the objects from the below graph, draw a "✓" in the column next to it. At the end of the trip have a look and see what you saw the most of and what you saw the least amount of times.

	1	2	3	4	5	6	7	8	9	10
 🚕										
 ⛽										
 🚲										
 🛑										
 🌴										
 🚦										
 ✈️										
 🧯										

travel
word puzzle

Unscramble the letters to spell each word.

R C A
☐ ☐ ☐

S A G S L S E
☐ ☐ ☐ ☐ ☐ ☐ ☐

P M A
☐ ☐ ☐

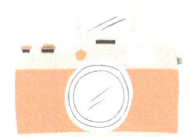

R C E M A A
☐ ☐ ☐ ☐ ☐ ☐

E A N I A L P R
☐ ☐ ☐ ☐ ☐ ☐ ☐ ☐

E L G A G U G
☐ ☐ ☐ ☐ ☐ ☐ ☐